# TIGERS BE STILL

## BY KIM ROSENSTOCK

★

★

DRAMATISTS
PLAY SERVICE
INC.

TIGERS BE STILL
Copyright © 2013, Kim Rosenstock

All Rights Reserved

**SPECIAL NOTE**

The following acknowledgments must appear in all programs distributed in connection with performances of the Play:

"Danger Zone"
(Giorgio Moroder and Tom Whitlock)
© 1986 WB Music Corp. (ASCAP)
and Famous Music Corporation (ASCAP)
All rights reserved. Used by permission.

"Take My Breath Away"
(Giorgio Moroder and Tom Whitlock)
© 1986 WB Music Corp. (ASCAP)
and Famous Music Corporation (ASCAP)
All rights reserved. Used by permission.

"The Rose"
(Amanda McBroom)
© 1977 Warner-Tamerlane Publishing Corp. (BMI)
and Third Story Music, Inc. (ASCAP)
All rights administered by Warner-Tamerlane Publishing Corp.
All rights reserved. Used by permission.

### SPECIAL NOTE ON SONGS

An additional fee of $30.00 per nonprofessional performance is required for use of the songs "Danger Zone," "Take My Breath Away," and "The Rose."

### SPECIAL NOTE ON SONGS AND RECORDINGS

For performances of copyrighted songs, arrangements or recordings mentioned in this Play, the permission of the copyright owner(s) must be obtained. Other songs, arrangements or recordings may be substituted provided permission from the copyright owner(s) of such songs, arrangements or recordings is obtained; or songs, arrangements or recordings in the public domain may be substituted.

*This play is for my mom.*

# SPECIAL THANKS

*Special thanks* to Dan Burson, Josh Chapman, Liz Engelman, Larnelle Foster, Gregg Henry, Portia Krieger, Cynthia Levin, Richard Nelson, Suzy Quinn, Karen & Michael Rosenstock, Megan Sandberg-Zakian, Shawny Sena, Lisa Timmel, Paula Vogel, Gavin Witt and Derek Zasky.

*A very special thanks* to all of the fantastic actors who brought the characters in this play to life in reading and workshop settings. And to all the stage managers who dealt with my neverending stream of new pages with infinite patience and grace.

*A very very special thanks* to the wonderful Roundabout Underground family, especially Todd Haimes, Robyn Goodman, Josh Fiedler and Jill Rafson.

# A NOTE ABOUT JOY

When I started this play, I was setting out to investigate the ways people locate joy in their lives during dark times. At some point I realized that I was writing a comedy about depression. And I decided that in order to maintain the comedic tone, there could only be a handful of moments in which the characters allowed themselves to stare directly into the void. I believe these "void moments" only have space to land when an effortful search for joy surrounds them.

# PRODUCTION NOTES

**Costumes:**
Grace should wear the same sweatsuit in every scene.

**Pre-Show:**
I always wanted the show to begin with a moment where the audience could observe Sherry and watch her make the decision to start telling her story. One example is the pre-show Sam Gold created for the Roundabout production. As the audience took their seats, Sherry was onstage, seated at her dining room table, putting the finishing touches on her model popsicle stick house. The audience watched her work. Then, when it came time to start, she finished what she was doing and began to speak.

**Scene Titles:**
A few directors have asked me whether or not I intended the scene titles to be displayed in production. The answer is: It didn't cross my mind. I originally wrote the titles to help me easily recall what happened in each scene. I realize this explanation is uninspired. I only offer it up because I feel bad when I think about some nice person working on this show spending any amount of his/her time trying to figure out what I intended.

**Sound:**
In the Roundabout production it proved helpful to hear recordings of Joseph making announcements over the school PA system as transitions into Scenes 8 and 15. I've included the text of these optional announcements in an appendix.

**Speech:**

A slash ( / ) in a sentence indicates where the next line begins to overlap with it.

**Wanda:**

In the Roundabout production, we could hear Wanda's voice on the other end of the phone whenever she called Sherry or Grace. The sound design was very realistic, so it was nearly impossible to make out exactly what she was saying. But intelligibility wasn't important. What was important was just knowing that she was there. I've included a map of Wanda's side of the phone conversations in an appendix.

TIGERS BE STILL was presented by Roundabout Theatre Company (Todd Haimes, Artistic Director; Harold Wolpert, Managing Director; Julia C. Levy, Executive Director) at the Black Box Theater at the Harold and Miriam Steinberg Center for Theatre in New York City, opening on October 6, 2010. It was directed by Sam Gold; the set design and costume designs were by Dane Laffrey; the lighting design was by Japhy Weideman; the sound design was by Fitz Patton; and the production stage manager was Kyle Gates. The cast was as follows:

SHERRY ................................ Halley Feiffer
JOSEPH ................................ Reed Birney
ZACK ................................. John Magaro
GRACE ............................... Natasha Lyonne


TIGERS BE STILL was first developed in the summer of 2008 at the MFA Playwrights' Workshop, produced in association with National New Play Network, at the Kennedy Center.


The play was subsequently developed in the spring of 2010 in a professional workshop at Portland Stage Company in Portland, Maine.

# CHARACTERS

SHERRY, 24

JOSEPH, 50

ZACK, 18

GRACE, 29

# PLACE

Present day.

# TIME

In a suburban town near a zoo.

# TIGERS BE STILL

## Scene 1

## The First Day

*We are in a suburban living room.*

*In the center of the room there's a large couch covered with tissues and candy wrappers. In front of the couch is a television. Behind the couch is a door with a padlock.*

*There is a staircase leading to a second floor.*

*Items in the living room include a coffee table, a telephone, an array of video game systems, a karaoke machine and shopping bags filled to the brim.*

*Sherry stands in the middle of the room, framed in a spotlight. She has an upbeat but slightly nervous energy. She's never done this before.*

SHERRY. This is the story of ... well ... I guess ... OK. This is the story of how I stopped being a total disaster and got my life on track and did *not* let overwhelming feelings of anxiousness and loneliness and uselessness just like totally eat my brain. I hope it will be an inspirational tale of triumph! *(Pause.)* I need to tell you a few things before we get started. First, my name is Sherry. And I'm twenty-four years old. And this is my home. *Welcome!* I live here with my mother and sister. And for the past month all three of us have just been sitting in here, depressed. And that's *bad*. But today is *good!* Because today I'm getting out of the house. Because

*today* I start my very first job. As an art teacher! In a school! And the first thing that happens at my first job is an emergency assembly. *(Joseph enters. He's distressed. He speaks into a microphone.)*
JOSEPH. *(Testing the mic.)* Check one. Check one.
SHERRY. The assembly is called by my first boss, Principal Moore, in order to alert everyone that —
JOSEPH. This morning a tiger escaped from the zoo. Officials have told us that this tiger could be anywhere within a hundred-mile radius. Since this town is within one mile of the zoo, that places us well within the range of "extreme danger." Here are the things I know about tigers: they are fast, they are big, they are mean and they have stripes. OK. So the question is: What is Oceanside Middle School doing to protect you, the student body? Well, we have cancelled recess indefinitely. P.E. classes will focus on indoor sports: basketball, and the other ones. Furthermore, we have three highly trained policemen who will be standing guard outside the school on lookout. We also have three highly trained lunch monitors who will be on lookout inside the school, in case the tiger comes to the cafeteria. And finally, we have instituted a school-wide buddy system so that everyone is accountable to at least one other person. *(A question is asked.)* What's that? Oh. No, I don't have a buddy. I have a rifle. Any other questions? OK … Then, uh, have a good day. And try to carry on like normal. *(Joseph exits. Sherry turns her attention back to the audience.)*
SHERRY. Principal Moore didn't just hire me to work at his school, he also hired me to work one-on-one with his son, Zack. *(Zack enters wearing a CVS shirt.)* Zack works at CVS. *(He holds up a box of tampons. He tries to swipe them at his register but he gets an "error" noise. He makes an angry sound.)* Zack has anger management issues. *(Zack addresses a customer in a deadpan manner.)*
ZACK. Oh. This box won't scan. Would you mind getting a new one? *(Pause.)* Yeah, I'm sure you know how much they cost, but I need to swipe it. *(Pause.)* It's not that I don't trust you, this isn't an issue of trust, it's an issue of store policy. *(Getting annoyed.)* Fine. Fine. *(Zack gets on his intercom.)* Maribel, I'm gonna need a price check up here on these extra-large, odor-protectant tampons. In case you missed that, that's *extra, large, odor, protectant, tampons.* That's *gigantic tampons* that have deodorant in them. For the lovely lady standing at the register in the purple hat. *(Zack glares at the customer and exits.)*

SHERRY. This is my sister Grace. *(Grace enters wearing a sweatsuit and holding a bottle of Jack Daniels. She's pretty drunk.)* Grace just got out of a long-term relationship and it was not her decision.

GRACE. Huh?

SHERRY. *(To Grace.)* Hey, Grace.

GRACE. *(Looking at the audience.)* What's going on?

SHERRY. I really need Grace to get off the couch for my first appointment with Zack. But when I ask her, "Grace, can you please get off the couch?" She tells me — *(Grace lies down on the couch, dramatically.)*

GRACE. I wish I could but I can't because I have lost the ability to move.

SHERRY. *(Sherry picks up a spice rack from the floor.)* Well you must have been moving at some point today because I see you made another trip to Troy's condo to steal something random.

GRACE. That's not random, that's a spice rack. And I didn't steal it, I earned it.

SHERRY. *(Sherry begins the Herculean task of cleaning the room — moving around in a straightening-up frenzy.)* Right. Look. Like I've said, I totally understand your impulse to take Troy's stuff / but —

GRACE. Do you think I should sleep with Mr. Cooper?

SHERRY. The mailman?

GRACE. You think he's cute?

SHERRY. I think he's old.

GRACE. I just figure it's time to try a real man, y'know, someone who's *really lived.* We got to talking today and it turns out we have a lot in common actually, like, we both love reading other people's mail, and smoothies. *(Grace turns on the television. She gets very excited.)* Oh, I love this show!

SHERRY. This is an adult diaper / commercial.

GRACE. Shhhh! It's the episode with the crossing guard.

SHERRY. Grace, he'll be here any minute. We need to straighten up!

GRACE. In a second, the end is the best part — she gets the diapers and then all of her grandkids gather around her while she helps them cross the street. See, look! *(We hear a crowd of kids cheering from the television.)* They're so happy to see that she can work again.

SHERRY. Could you maybe try to get all of the tissues and candy wrappers off the couch? This is no longer just a living room, it's a home office. *(Grace turns the television off.)*

GRACE. Why do you get to have a home office? Maybe I need this to be *my* home office. Maybe it already is.

SHERRY. I'm just trying to my make my patient feel comfortable and welcome.

GRACE. Well, I'm sorry but I can't let you have the couch. I need it.

SHERRY. And you can have it, except for on Tuesdays at 4 P.M. when I use it for therapy. Which is right now. I'm trying to be calm but I told you about it this morning and you had all day to make this room presentable. I wanted everything to be perfect. Principal Moore can't know that his son is my first patient.

GRACE. *(Sighing heavily.)* Fine. *(Starts to clean up the tissues and candy wrappers.)* But I'm not bothering with the ones that are underneath the cushions. *(Grace pushes a bunch of stuff under the cushions.)*

SHERRY. I just want things to go well, you know — it's just uncertain right now whether or not this job is gonna be like a permanent thing. I have to prove myself if I want to get hired full-time … which would be, I mean just thinking about having a full-time job is … *thrilling.*

GRACE. You need a boyfriend, so badly.

SHERRY. No I don't.

GRACE. This twenty-four-year streak is a real accomplishment, don't get me wrong. But enough is enough. You need to go to a bar. Or a website. Or maybe your patient could be your boyfriend. I mean, clearly you're trying hard to impress him.

SHERRY. I'm not trying to impress him. I'm trying to seem professional. I'm trying to *not* seem like a therapist whose home office is a dirty couch that smells like tears.

GRACE. I bet he's gonna be hot. I mean, we know his dad was a total fox. That picture of him in Mom's room is just like … Ugh. It's sad to think that someone that hot has to get old, you know? And it's like, good for Mom, dating a hot guy. But then it's like, stupid Mom, for marrying a plain-looking man and having only reasonably attractive children. If Mom had stayed with that guy — the one in that picture — we would be *hot.*

SHERRY. We wouldn't exist.

GRACE. Whatever, *Darwin.*

SHERRY. Besides, we *are* hot.

GRACE. I'm sorry to break it to you Li'l / Sis —

SHERRY. Don't call me / Li'l Sis.

GRACE. — but the proof is in the pudding. Where are our boyfriends? Hot girls have boyfriends.

SHERRY. You should know that you have a habit of saying completely untrue things like they're facts.

GRACE. What's your patient's name?

SHERRY. Zack.

GRACE. I say you make Sack your boyfriend.

SHERRY. *Zack* is eighteen years old *and* he's my first patient. So, in conclusion, dating him is the stupidest thing I could do.

GRACE. There's often a fine line between the stupidest thing you could do and *the sexiest thing you could do.*

SHERRY. Like sleeping with the seventy-five-year-old mailman?

GRACE. Perfect example.

SHERRY. Grace, promise me you won't do that.

GRACE. Why? You've been on my case about being more active. Fucking Mr. Cooper would feel very active.

SHERRY. You know what else would feel active? Returning all of Troy's stuff before he presses charges. I bet that would feel active. *(Behind the door, the muffled sound of dogs barking is heard. Sherry looks at the door, startled. Then she turns toward Grace who looks guilty, but also delighted.)*

GRACE. Umm … yeah, sooo —

SHERRY. Dogs?! *(Sherry follows the sound of the dogs over to the door. She tries to open it but she can't. She discovers the padlock.)* Why is there a padlock on the basement door? *(Realizing.)* Oh no … *Grace, NO!* I told you not to do this! We talked about it and everything. We made a pros and cons list!

GRACE. *Rage* can't be divided into pros and cons. Ooh, shhh, listen. *(The sound of claws on the door.)* It sounds like they're trying to break the door down with their little useless paws. Ha! This one time when Troy and I were lying in bed just like talking about our lives, one of those *creatures* jumped on my face and its like, its *anus* ended up on top of my eye. Have you ever had an *anus on your eye?* Well *I have.* Then the other one put his paw on my mouth as if to shush me! Tell me that wasn't premeditated, OK? Those little motherfuckers are pathological.

SHERRY. Troy must be a wreck.

GRACE. Oh, I hadn't thought about that — do you think Troy's going through a *hard time? Because that would just be awful.*

SHERRY. This is cruel, Grace.

GRACE. It's not cruel. They're beasts.

SHERRY. They're chihuahuas!

GRACE. You know, you've become awfully judgmental ever since Mom got you this job. I liked you better when you were unemployed, you were more mellow.

SHERRY. I was paralyzed with depression.

GRACE. You were a great listener. Look. After everything Troy did to me, I'm allowed to seek my revenge. I was *planning a wedding for fuck's sake.* If he wants the dogs back, he can man up, come over here and get them. And when he does he's finally going to have to *deal with me.* He's going to have to *wet himself with remorse before he ever lays eyes on those little bastards ever again!*

SHERRY. Do you really think it's worth it? Doing all this just to see him?

GRACE. Y'know, just because you're suddenly all *functional,* doesn't mean you won't hit rock bottom again. You could fall back into the shit at any moment. And when you do I'll be here, waiting for you.

SHERRY. Thank you, that's beautiful.

GRACE. Thank you. *(Grace begins to lie back down on the couch. The doorbell rings. The dogs start barking.)*

SHERRY. Grace, please? *(Grace sighs and gets up, dramatically.)*

GRACE. OK, I'll move. This time. But just know that I really like the couch and I really resent having to relocate. And if I see Troy's car pull up, I'm coming back down and shit's gonna get crazy. *(Grace heads up the stairs.)*

SHERRY. *(Sherry takes a deep breath and opens the door. Zack stands in the doorway.)* Hi!

ZACK. Hey, I'm Zack.

SHERRY. I know. I'm Sherry. This is my home. *Welcome! (Pause.)* Please, come in. *(Zack enters.)* Just have a seat in my office. *(Sherry gestures to the couch. They sit down. Bette Midler's "The Rose" starts playing from upstairs. Sherry hands Zack a notebook.)* So this is for you. I thought we'd / start with —

ZACK. Where's that music coming from?

SHERRY. *(Casual.)* Oh from my sister's room. She's a big Bette Midler fan. Anyway — *(From offstage Grace lets out a loud sobbing noise.)*

ZACK. Is she crying?

16

SHERRY. No, I think she's singing.

ZACK. It sounds like she's —

GRACE. *(Offstage.)* Ugghh!!! *(There is a crashing sound and the music stops abruptly.)*

SHERRY. Anyway, I made an agenda for this meeting. *(Sherry hands Zack the agenda.)* And the first thing on the list is finding out a little more about you. I know you work at CVS, what's that like?

ZACK. Incredible.

SHERRY. And you are taking a year off between high school and college which is not that uncommon. *(Zack: … )* And I know you like rap music which is really funny because *I* like rap music.

ZACK. Oh yeah, who do you listen to?

SHERRY. And your dad told me you also really like comic books.

ZACK. Just *The Hulk*. What is this notebook?

SHERRY. It's not a notebook, it's your artist's journal. For your thoughts and drawings.

ZACK. My what?

SHERRY. See, at the end of each session, I'll give you an assignment — something to write about and to draw in the journal and then you'll hand it in to me at the next meeting. This way we can track our progress.

ZACK. Why do I need a journal to be your assistant teacher?

SHERRY. Oh no, sorry, this is a journal for our sessions.

ZACK. Our sessions?

SHERRY. Didn't your father explain?

ZACK. Yeah. He said I was going to be your assistant teacher. He thinks my CVS job is bullshit. So he said I had to do a non-bullshit job to balance it out.

SHERRY. So he didn't tell you about the therapy?

ZACK. *(Eyes widening.)* No.

SHERRY. Ah. *(To herself.)* That's unfortunate … *(Zack just stares at her.)* OK. SO. "The deal" is … So part of my job is to work with you in the classroom and part of my job is to help rehabilitate you — outside of the classroom. *(Proudly.)* I'm an art therapist, Zack. And this is our first art therapy session. *(Zack puts his head in his hands and makes a strange sound.)* Um, are you OK?

ZACK. *(Not looking up.)* Yeah, sometimes I can feel my brain trying to flee my skull. It's nothing. Continue.

SHERRY. He said he was going to tell you. Your father. He said you knew. Why did you think you were here?

17

ZACK. I don't know. To go over like lesson plans or something? Not for *art therapy*. I didn't even know that was an actual thing until just now.

SHERRY. Oh, OK. Well, l just wanted to say that I've worked on some other grief cases but I'm particularly excited to get to work with you because I think we're going to do a lot of great work together.

ZACK. You just said "work" three times in one sentence.

SHERRY. Anyway, I'm —

ZACK. Are you my age?

SHERRY. I'm older than you.

ZACK. You look really young.

SHERRY. *(Psyching herself up.)* So yeah! OK! I guess we can go over some lesson plans first. For the next month the students will be working on the popsicle stick house project! *(Sherry unveils a model popsicle stick house.)*

ZACK. That sounds horrible.

SHERRY. Well it's actually *pretty cool. (Sherry gives Zack a handful of popsicle sticks.)* Here are some popsicle sticks for you to take home with you. Now, uh … I want you to come up with an addition to the popsicle stick house project — something you can show the kids how to make. Like maybe a popsicle stick fence? Or a popsicle stick garage? But I don't want to influence you, so come up with your own creation! You know, something / that —

ZACK. *(Rising.)* I'm sorry, I've gotta get to CVS.

SHERRY. Oh, OK. Uh, can I just give you a quick journal assignment / before you —

ZACK. *(Heading for the door.)* My shift starts in ten minutes. If I'm late they get really annoying.

SHERRY. Alright. Well then, I guess, can you just tell me what you see in these — these … *(Sherry rifles through her papers and holds up some ink blots.)* I just want to have something in case your father wants some proof that we're actually doing the therapy stuff.

ZACK. How many cards are there?

SHERRY. Um, ten.

ZACK. *(Zack rattles off ten things without looking at the ink blots.)* Death. My mom. A horse. Christmas day. Spoons. Baby carrots. A rifle. The night sky. A sea otter.

SHERRY. *(Writing frantically.)* That's only nine.

ZACK. Hockey.

SHERRY. Stick? Puck? Game?

ZACK. Just hockey. *(Zack exits.)*

SHERRY. *(Shouting after him.)* Good first session! *(To herself.)* Even if it was only … *(She checks the time.)* four minutes long … *(Sherry sits for a moment and stares at her agenda. The house phone rings and she picks it up.)* Hi Mom. *(Pause.)* It went OK, I guess. *(Pause.)* Yeah. I saw him at this assembly about the tiger that escaped from the local zoo. *(Pause.)* Blonde and wavy? Not exactly, kind of thin and grayish?* *(Pause.)* I'm actually supposed to meet with him tomorrow. *(Pause.)* OK, I'll tell him. Hey, so *Jeopardy*'s on — you want to challenge me? I'll go easy on you this time. *(Pause.)* OK, alright … sure you don't need anything? I can come upstairs and — *(Pause.)* OK, no, I know, I just thought, you know, in honor of my first day of work but — *(Pause.)* I know, it's OK. (pause.) Yeah, I'll tell him. *(Pause.)* I'll remember. *(Pause.)* Bye.

## Scene 2

## When All of the Women were in Bed

*Sherry addresses the audience.*

SHERRY. Exactly one month ago all of the women in my family were in bed. All the time. "How does this happen?" Here's how. About a year ago, my mom stopped getting out of bed. Several months later, I followed. And a month ago, my sister joined in. *(Grace enters holding a picture of Troy.)* This is Troy. Troy and Grace were engaged to be married until a month ago when Grace caught him cheating on her with his podiatrist, Dr. Carol. After that she —

GRACE. I'm sorry. I really need to say a few things about Troy.

SHERRY. Will it make you feel better?

GRACE. Yes.

SHERRY. Then, sure / I guess …

GRACE. Troy sells insurance. Troy loves his dogs. Troy doesn't believe in "Valentine's Day" or "birthdays" or "mutual orgasms" or

---

* This line can be altered to fit the description of the actor playing Joseph.

"jewelry." But he believes passionately in giving gag gifts. On our fourth anniversary I bought him a watch with the words "Forever your girl" engraved on the back. He got me this book called *Everyone Poops. (Grace holds up her copy of* Everyone Poops.*)* Yeah. It's just like — *what the fuck am I supposed to do with this book?* Troy loves camping but I could never go with him because I refuse to poop anywhere that is *not* a bathroom.

SHERRY. Anyway, the / good news —

GRACE. I bet Dr. Carol loves camping. I bet Dr. Carol and Troy are shitting in the woods together right now!

SHERRY. The good news is that this past week Grace moved from the bed to the couch, which was a big step. *(Grace sits on the couch and rips the picture of Troy in half.)*

GRACE. Ahhh!

SHERRY. *(Nurturing.)* Are you done?

GRACE. *(Quietly.)* Yes.

SHERRY. And that's pretty much where she spends most of her waking hours. On the couch, watching the same movie over and over again. *(Grace picks up a remote control and presses play.)* And that movie is: *Top Gun. (The theme song from Top Gun plays.)* She'll watch the whole thing. But often she'll just turn it to this one part. She knows exactly where it is.

GRACE. Fifty-three minutes, thirty-three seconds in. *("Take My Breath Away" plays.)*

SHERRY. It's the love scene.

GRACE. *(Grace gazes at the television longingly.)* It's romantic and sensual and when I watch him slowly put his tongue on top of her tongue again and again … I feel alive …

SHERRY. Hey, it's progress. On the other hand … *(She gestures upstairs.)* There's our mom: Wanda. Last fall she got sick with this auto-immune disease. And her doctor put her on this medication. But the medication made her like, gain all of this weight? And, after a while she didn't want anyone to look at her anymore. So she stopped leaving her bedroom. The only person she would let see her was my dad. And then one day she stopped letting my dad in. And a few days after she stopped letting him in, he left. Just … disappeared. *(Sherry tries to lighten the mood.)* And then there's me! This past January I earned my master's degree in art therapy. I sent out fifty resumes and cover letters. And *nothing.* I ended up at home with nowhere to go and nothing to do. So I figured I'd just get some reading done. Just sit in my childhood bed and read for a while. And pretty soon, I was just sitting in bed *not* reading. Just sitting. I was sitting in bed when Grace moved back home. I was sitting in bed when my dad left. And I was sitting in bed when my mom called me to say she had gotten me a job. *A job.* And what's amazing is that the moment I found out I had that job — *the instant I found out* — it was like for the first time I wasn't terrified of putting my feet on the ground. *(Triumphantly.)* And *that's* The Story Of How I Got Out Of Bed.

## Scene 3

## The Basketball Hoop

*The next day.*

*Sherry and Zack stand in front of their students.*

*Zack is wearing a button-down shirt and a tie.*

SHERRY. Alright everyone, listen up! Mr. Moore is going to show you how to make a popsicle stick basketball hoop!

ZACK. *(Zack goes through the following demonstration with extreme difficulty. It's painful for him.)* So, you take a popsicle stick and you break it at a ninety-degree angle at the base like this ... *(Zack breaks a popsicle stick at the base.)* And then you attach these little paper baskets we have to the top of the popsicle stick. *(Zack puts a paper basket on the stick.)* And then you just, you know ... you put it in your popsicle stick driveway. And you can wad up a little ball of orange tissue paper and put it in the basket — *(Zack takes a tiny ball of orange tissue paper out of his pocket and holds it up.)* That's your basketball.

SHERRY. Isn't that great? He really used his imagination. I want to see all of you doing the same.

ZACK. Yeah, you too can make something like this. *(Zack holds up the popsicle stick basketball hoop. It looks really shabby.)*

SHERRY. Thank you, Mr. Moore. Now, I'm —

ZACK. Hey, raise your hand if you want to go on a field trip to the basketball court for research purposes. *(Zack raises his own hand and surveys the classroom.)* Nice.

SHERRY. *(Flustered but chipper.)* You can all put your hands down. Now. Thank you, Mr. Moore.

ZACK. Any time.


## Scene 4

## Pep Talk


*Later that afternoon.*

*Joseph sits at his desk eating a sandwich. There's a knock on the door.*


JOSEPH. Come in! *(Sherry enters. Joseph drops his sandwich and stares at her.)*

SHERRY. Hi, I'm Sherry Wickman, Wanda's daughter?

JOSEPH. You look like her. That's amazing. *(He extends his hand.)* Joseph Moore, nice to meet you. I wanted to introduce myself, check in … So? How are the little animals?

SHERRY. *(Paranoid.)* How do you know about that?

JOSEPH. What?

SHERRY. Oh, you mean the students! They're great!

JOSEPH. And my son?

SHERRY. Well, we just had our first class together and I think he's going to be a real … *presence.*

JOSEPH. Oh good. That's a relief. To be honest, I was more than a little worried this arrangement would completely blow up in my face! *(Reaching into his drawer.)* Butterscotch?

SHERRY. Sure. *(Joseph hands her a butterscotch which she unwraps and puts in her mouth.)* Also, we had a very productive first art therapy session yesterday in my home office.

JOSEPH. *(Surprised.)* You did?

SHERRY. Yes.

JOSEPH. Great. Well, thanks for taking him under your wing. I couldn't let him just sit around this year. That's not the way you get into SUNY Binghamton. My alma mater. It's the best SUNY. Also, this will help keep him off the streets. There's a tiger out there. And drug dealers. Say, did you get your buddy? I instituted a school-wide buddy system.

SHERRY. No.

JOSEPH. Let's make Zack your buddy then.

SHERRY. Oh. OK.

JOSEPH. Very good.

SHERRY. Oh, hey, my mom told me to tell you "Hi."

JOSEPH. *(Perking up.)* "Hi?"

SHERRY. Yes.

JOSEPH. Well. Tell your mother I said … "Hello."

SHERRY. OK.

JOSEPH. Your mother and I go way back, you know.

SHERRY. Yes, I've seen the prom picture.

JOSEPH. *(Amazed.)* She still has it?

SHERRY. Yes. She likes the way she looks in it. She looks like a princess. She even has her tiara.

JOSEPH. I have my crown!

SHERRY. Anyway, I know she appreciates this a lot. You giving me this opportunity. And you should know that I give every job 110% — but if for some reason you start to think that maybe I'm not the best person to work with Zack, I would completely understand / if —

JOSEPH. Oh *come on.* Have some confidence! What's with young people today not having confidence? It perplexcs me. Say, "I am Sherry Wickman and I am damn good at what I do." DAMN good. Punch the damn! Say it.

SHERRY. OK, can I say it in my mind?

JOSEPH. Nope, say it out loud.

SHERRY. Um, OK … I am Sherry Wickman and I am good / at —

JOSEPH. *(Shaking his head.)* Eh eh!

SHERRY. I am Sherry Wickman and I am DAMN good at what I do!

JOSEPH. That's better! Now hop to it! *(They high five and Sherry exits.)*

# Scene 5

## Dinnertime

*Later that evening.*

*Zack and Joseph sit at the dinner table eating lasagna. There is a television on nearby and Zack watches it intently as he moves his food around with his fork.*

JOSEPH. *(To Zack.)* Do you like it? I know it's your favorite so I tried to follow your mother's recipe. Only problem was I couldn't find basil leaves at the store, so I bought spinach instead. And I may have accidentally doubled the salt. What do you think? *(Zack is silent.)* So how's it going? Sherry's nice, huh? Are you enjoying working with her? Is it weird to hear the kids calling you "Mr. Moore"? I know it still sounds weird to me when I hear them call me that. But you get used to it. *(Zack is silent.)* I thought next week we could donate your mom's shoes somewhere. And then we could knock down the wall between her shoe closet and your room. Finally give you the big room you always wanted. You'd like that, right?

ZACK. Not really. *(Zack continues to stare at the television. Joseph eats.)*

JOSEPH. *(After a moment.)* This really would have been better with basil.

# Scene 6

## Some Say Love, It is a River.

*The following Tuesday. Early afternoon.*

*Grace sits on the couch in the dark. Curtains drawn. Her bottle of Jack is propped up next to her.*

*An instrumental version of "The Rose" plays on the karaoke machine. She picks up her cell phone, dials, and puts it on speakerphone.*

THE VOICE OF TROY. *(Through speakerphone.)* Hey, it's Troy. Leave a message and I'll call you back. Beeeeep. *(Beep.)*
GRACE. *(Sings into the phone.)*
  *Some say love, it is a river*
  *that drowns the tender reed.*
  *Some say love, it is a razor*
  *that leaves your soul to bleed.*
  *Some say love, it is a hunger,*
  *an endless aching need.*
  *I say love it is a flower,*
  *and you ASSHOLE its only seed.*
*(The house phone rings. "The Rose" continues to play out as Grace puts down her cell phone and picks up the home phone.)* Hi Mom. *(Pause.)* Oh, I was singing. *(Pause.)* Mom, can I come to your room? *(Pause.)* I won't look at you. I'll just lie down on the carpet. You won't even know I'm there. Please? *(Pause.)* OK … I'll keep it down. *(Grace hangs up the phone and curls up into the fetal position, using her bottle as a pillow.)*

# Scene 7

## Art Therapy

*Later that afternoon.*

*Sherry and Zack sit on the couch. Grace is on the end of the couch, sleeping.*

ZACK. Uh, should we go somewhere else?

SHERRY. Oh don't worry — she's fine.

ZACK. *(Getting a closer look.)* She's spooning a bottle of Jack Daniels.

SHERRY. Yes. OK, so I was thinking that we could start off this week's session with a very simple assignment for the journal.

ZACK. Can I give you some feedback on the class first?

SHERRY. Um ... well, / I —

ZACK. Look, this popsicle stick thing sucks. I think you've got to do something more fun or there's going to be an *uprising.*

SHERRY. I appreciate your feedback. Thank you. But I really don't think it's that bad. I think the kids are enjoying it.

ZACK. One kid fell asleep while gluing his popsicle stick roof together. That's how bored he was.

SHERRY. You're exaggerating.

ZACK. Sadly, no.

SHERRY. Well, I'm new to the whole teaching thing, so I'm hoping to get better, of course.

ZACK. Today three kids climbed out of the window and ran away while you were looking for your glasses in your purse. *(Smiles, remembering.)* I thought it was funny so I just waved goodbye.

SHERRY. You did?

ZACK. Yeah, I guess I'm a pretty bad assistant art teacher. I should retire. I'll tell my dad. He'll be disappointed in me but, whatever.

SHERRY. Oh no, please don't do that. We're both new to this — we can get better.

ZACK. Look, I actually like my job at Walgreens better than

teaching that class, it's oddly more fulfilling.

SHERRY. Walgreens? I thought you worked at CVS.

ZACK. I got fired.

SHERRY. From CVS? How?

ZACK. I stole a candy out of one of those bins.

SHERRY. You stole?

ZACK. Yes, technically, but it's like, come on — I stand there ringing up tampons and smokes all day and I can't take a fucking caramel swirl? Anyway, it's OK because, I went across the street to Walgreens and they hired me *on the spot. (Sherry starts laughing.)* That's funny?

SHERRY. No, it's just … OK, so this is a little embarrassing but one summer between my junior and senior years of college, I tried to get a job — *any job.* I wanted desperately to be able to say to someone, "I've got to go to work …" or "Sorry, I can't make it until after work …" You know, like, stuff that working people say? Anyway, I applied everywhere — CVS and Walgreens included — and I gave them my resume along with a copy of my transcript — and I sat by my phone and waited and waited — and I never got a call from *any of them.*

ZACK. Did *you* ever call *them?*

SHERRY. No.

ZACK. Did you go inside and ask them to hire you?

SHERRY. Well, I filled out the application forms.

ZACK. Dude, you didn't show any follow-through initiative, no wonder they didn't hire you.

SHERRY. Are you serious?

ZACK. *(Amused.)* Yeah. You gave them your college transcript? That's retarded. Like they care if you've taken Greek Literature or whatever at Walgreens? All they care about is: are you not retarded. But once they saw that you gave them a resume and transcript they were probably like, "Nope, she doesn't meet our ONE qualification."

SHERRY. I think the hiring procedures were different back when I was applying, OK? More *cutthroat.*

ZACK. Whatever you need to tell yourself. *(Dogs bark. A beat.)* What's that?

SHERRY. *(Attempting to be nonchalant.)* Oh. Dogs.

ZACK. Are they in a closet / or something?

SHERRY. *(To herself.)* They're probably hungry. *(Sherry reaches over Zack and taps Grace to wake her up.)* Grace? *(Louder.)* Grace! Get up and feed the dogs! *(Like a zombie, Grace rises up. She hands Zack her bottle.)*

GRACE. Here.

ZACK. Um, I'm underage. This is a crime.

GRACE. *(Grace takes a few steps and stops, confused. looking around.)* What am I doing?

SHERRY. You're feeding the dogs!

GRACE. Correct! *(Grace gets a big bag of dog food, takes a handful and pushes it under the door.)* Here! Dinner! *(The dogs are heard hungrily gobbling up the food. Grace goes back to her spot on the couch. She eyes Sherry and Zack suspiciously.)* You two better not be making out on this couch while I'm sleeping.

ZACK. What?

GRACE. You heard me ... *(Grace goes back to sleep with her bottle.)*

SHERRY. Sorry, she's inappropriate.

ZACK. Why do you keep your dogs locked in a closet?

SHERRY. That's not a closet, that's the basement. And they're not my dogs, they're my sister's dogs. Well they're not her dogs, they're Troy's dogs.

ZACK. Who the fuck is Troy?

SHERRY. Her ex-fiancé. He cheated on her with his podiatrist, Dr. Carol. She caught them making out over a plate of quesadillas at Applebee's. She threw a glass at them and Applebee's called the authorities. It's been a while, about a month, you know, and she's been trying to get her life back on track but it's been hard. And she's been stealing his things. And his dogs. Look, this is like part of some healing process she needs to go through, OK? You understand that, right?

ZACK. I understand that this is *a kidnapping!* And you're totally an accomplice or like an accessory, or both, I think you're both! *(The house phone rings. Sherry looks at it — she's not sure whether or not to get it. It keeps ringing. Zack stares at her, then the phone, then her, then the phone, then her ... )* Are you gonna answer that?

SHERRY. *(Hesitating.)* Umm ... *(Brightly.)* Yeah, OK! Just gimme a second. *(Into the phone.)* Hi, Mom! Is everything OK? *(Pause. Zack looks at his watch.)*

ZACK. Shit, I gotta get to work. *(Zack begins to gather his stuff. Sherry motions for him to wait a moment. Zack lingers.)*

SHERRY. *(Into the phone.)* Oh. Um, yeah, I'm going tonight actually. Do you want the usual stuff or something different? *(Pause.)* Bananas. *(Pause.)* And English muffins. Got it. *(Pause.)* Cinammon raisin. Got it. *(Pause.)* Whole wheat. OK ... Um, Mom, I'm kind of working right now. But can I call you back in a little bit? *(Pause.)* OK. *(Sherry hangs up and sees Zack looking at her.)*

ZACK. You do your mom's grocery shopping?

SHERRY. Well, I do the shopping for the household. My mom lives upstairs. She's just in her room.

ZACK. *(Looking up, surprised.)* Like, right now?

SHERRY. Uh ... yeah.

ZACK. And she calls you in your own house? Why doesn't she come down?

SHERRY. *(Casually.)* Oh. Because she can't. I mean, well, she hasn't. In a while.

ZACK. That's ...

SHERRY. Weird?

ZACK. *(Zack stares at Sherry for a quick moment.)* Yeah.

SHERRY. *(Uncomfortable.)* Well, you've gotta get to work, right?

ZACK. Yeah. See you tomorrow.

SHERRY. *(Sherry claps her hands with joy and jumps.)* Yes! I knew you weren't really going to retire!

ZACK. *(Moving towards the door.)* OK ...

SHERRY. Hey wait ... Journal assignment: draw a house. *(Zack nods and exits.)*


## Scene 8

## The Pond


*The following Tuesday at the school. Sherry and Joseph sit in his office. Joseph looks very annoyed.*


SHERRY. *(Shaken up.)* I can explain! See, it was such a nice day outside and the pond is so close by. I thought it would be a nice little change of pace and maybe you know, like more … fun?

JOSEPH. *Fun?*

SHERRY. Yes.

JOSEPH. Do you know that tigers love ponds?

SHERRY. They do?

JOSEPH. *Who knows? BUT THEY MIGHT!* Sherry — didn't you hear the lunch monitors yelling at you to come back?

SHERRY. I didn't realize they were screaming at me. I thought they were screaming about … *(Weakly.)* lunch?

JOSEPH. You put an entire class of children in danger. You broke a major school policy.

SHERRY. *(Beginning to cry.)* I'm so sorry. I didn't realize — I swear — it was just the town pond … Am I being fired?

JOSEPH. Oh, wait, don't, don't do that. *(Joseph reaches for a Kleenex.)* Kleenex? *(Sherry takes it and blows her nose.)*

SHERRY. I didn't want to endanger the students! I feel so stupid!

JOSEPH. I'm going to give you a second chance, you know. So just calm down.

SHERRY. You are?

JOSEPH. Yes, I am. And do you know why?

SHERRY. Why?

JOSEPH. Because Zack told me that you're a very good therapist.

SHERRY. Really? I mean, um, yes it's been going well.

JOSEPH. Has he talked about the shoe closet yet?

SHERRY. No. Is that a closet just for shoes?

JOSEPH. Yes.

SHERRY. Wow, I've never seen an *entire closet just for shoes.*

JOSEPH. It was my wife's.

SHERRY. Oh …

JOSEPH. Ever since she died, Zack does this thing where he sits in there for hours. He thinks I don't know where he is. But I know. Last night he'd been in there for a long time and so I knocked on the door. Finally, after getting no answer, I opened the door and I found him on the floor of the closet asleep. His face was inside one of her tennis shoes as though he'd been smelling it. *(Joseph stares off for a moment.)*

SHERRY. Um …

JOSEPH. *(Composing himself.)* You'll ask him about it then?

SHERRY. Yes.

JOSEPH. Very good. *(Sherry gets up to leave.)* Oh, and did you

give your mother my message?
SHERRY. Your message?
JOSEPH. Yes, you remember? *"Hello."*
SHERRY. Ah, right. No, I forgot.
JOSEPH. *(Upset.)* You forgot?
SHERRY. But I'll tell her tonight.
JOSEPH. Great. And Sherry, no more field trips, OK? Remember: there's plenty to see *inside* the school.
SHERRY. Right. Got it. *(Sherry exits.)*

## Scene 9

## The Rescue: Part 1

*Later that afternoon.*

*Lights come up on Zack and Sherry sitting on the couch. Grace is once again at the end, sleeping. The Top Gun theme song can be heard coming from the television.*

ZACK. *(Gesturing to Grace.)* Look at her. It's the middle of the afternoon.
SHERRY. *(Looking at Grace.)* I think she's getting better. I know it's hard to tell but —
ZACK. She's sleeping. And drinking. *(Impressed.)* She's sleep-drinking!
SHERRY. OK, we should start our session. *(Sherry shuts off the movie.)*
ZACK. Class today was better. I thought the pond field trip was a big success.
SHERRY. Of course you did. *(The dogs bark. Zack moves to the closet.)*
ZACK. You know, I've been thinking about this. We could get them out of there. I'm kind of an expert lock-picker.
SHERRY. Really?

ZACK. Yeah. Usually I charge for my services, but they're free for friends and family.

SHERRY. So I'm your friend?

ZACK. It's just an expression.

SHERRY. I'm not your family, so I must be your friend. You said it and you can't take it back. Sorry.

ZACK. Just … give me your hair clip.

SHERRY. OK, *friend. (Sherry gives him her hair clip. Zack crosses back to the lock and begins to tinker with it. Sherry follows.)* Let's do this! Ooh! Picking a lock! This is fun! It's like a top secret mission! Like we're spies!

ZACK. *(Concentrating.)* Now, this will just take a second …

SHERRY. Sooo. Did you do the journal assignment from last week? You know — drawing the house?

ZACK. No.

SHERRY. *(Disappointed.)* Oh. Well —

ZACK. *(Growing frustrated with the lock.)* Shit, why isn't this working?

SHERRY. It's just that — you need to draw things or, I can't really — *(Zack smacks the lock angrily.)*

ZACK. *Shit!* I think your sister like pick-proofed this lock or something. Unbelievable. Do you have a hammer?

SHERRY. A hammer? Yes! We have many tools … In the basement.

ZACK. *(Suddenly furious.)* Shit! That *sucks! (Zack throws the hairpin across the room.)*

SHERRY. Woah, calm down. *(Zack punches the wall. He hurts his hand.)*

ZACK. Ow!

SHERRY. Are you OK?

ZACK. Yeah.

SHERRY. Zack? *(Zack gathers his things quickly and heads for the door.)*

ZACK. Sorry. I didn't mean to scare you.

SHERRY. You don't have to apologize. Are you leaving? We haven't done any work yet.

ZACK. I've gotta run home.

SHERRY. Why?

ZACK. *(Running out.)* Don't worry, I'll be back! *(Zack exits. Sherry goes to the couch and covers Grace with a blanket. She sits down next to her. The phone rings.)*

SHERRY. *(Into the phone.)* Hi, Mom. How are you? *(Pause.)* Oh, really? Well we've got some antacid down here — do you want me to bring it in to you? *(Pause.)* OK, I'll slide it under. Hey, I've officially been employed for two weeks. Pretty great, huh? *(Pause.)* She's here with me. *(Pause.)* She's sleeping. *(Pause.)* Uh, she's looked better. But I think she could kill a lot of birds with one shower. *(Pause.)* Um, so look … we really miss you, Mom. I know I've said this before but … We don't care what you look like. You know that. We just want you to come downstairs. *(Pause.)* Oh, yeah, I told him. He says, "Hello." *(Pause.)* Yeah, that's it. *(Pause.)* "Harold Ashman's pants?" — what does that mean? *(Pause. )* OK, I'll just tell him. *(Pause. Sherry chuckles.)* OK. Bye.

## Scene 10

### The Story of Wanda and Joseph

*Sherry and Zack stand on stage. Zack wears a crown and 1970s tuxedo jacket and shirt. Sherry wears a wig or something to indicate that she is playing the part of her mother.*

*Note: this scene should have the feel of a short play that Sherry wrote and is making Zack perform. Zack's performance should feel a little stiff.*

SHERRY. This is the story of my mom — Wanda. And Principal Moore —
ZACK. Joseph.
SHERRY. As kids, Wanda and Joseph lived one street apart and went to the same school. They watched each other grow up. Of course they couldn't really tell that's what they were doing since when you see someone every day it's hard to tell there's a change. And suddenly it seemed like he was five-foot-ten and she was a 32C.
ZACK. I had a paper route. And one day as I threw the morning

paper onto Wanda's family's lawn —

SHERRY. He accidentally threw the paper at my face.

ZACK. And she screamed at me:

SHERRY. "Watch where you throw that thing, Joe!" And then I rubbed my head and fixed my bra and went inside.

ZACK. And that's when I saw her bra strap. And from that moment forward I was *hooked*. It took a few weeks but I finally worked up the courage to ask her out. I had memorized exactly what I was going to say the night before just so I wouldn't mess it up. I meant to wait until we were alone, but the moment I saw her in home economics I blurted out, "Hello Wanda I'd like to you out to the movies this weekend if that's alright with you and your parents."

SHERRY. And I said, "I think you forgot a word."

ZACK. I mean — I'd like to *ask* / you —

SHERRY. Sure!

ZACK. And so it began.

SHERRY. We had our first date at the movies.

ZACK. We had our first kiss in the back of my dad's car.

SHERRY. We had our first fight in the middle of a thunderstorm.

ZACK. And we had our first well, *you know,* on my bedroom floor.

SHERRY. And afterwards we listened to The Beatles. *("Norwegian Wood" plays.)* And we lay there, not saying a word.

ZACK. Until she started to hum.

SHERRY. And then he started to hum. *(They hum.)* And his hair was wavy and blonde.

ZACK. And her skin glowed. *(Zack produces two crowns, and he puts one on himself and crowns Sherry with the other under the following.)* And on prom night we were crowned king and queen.

SHERRY. And after the prom, a bunch of us went back to my house. To the basement.

ZACK. And someone suggested spin the bottle.

SHERRY. And *that's* when he kissed Allison Goldstein.

ZACK. Because *those are the rules!*

SHERRY. I don't care about the rules!

ZACK. She refused to forgive me.

SHERRY. I refused to forgive him.

ZACK. She wouldn't even speak to me all summer.

SHERRY. Because I was stubborn.

ZACK. And then one day she left for college.

SHERRY. Without a word.

ZACK. And that's how it ended. *(Music stops.)*

SHERRY. And time passed.

ZACK. And they got older.

SHERRY. And no amount of Rogaine could stop his hair from falling out.

ZACK. And no amount of moisturizer could make her skin glow the way it used to.

SHERRY. It just made her pillow greasy.

ZACK. And even though they only lived two towns apart, their paths didn't cross for thirty-five years.

SHERRY. Until one day I decided to find him on the internet. And when I saw that he was the principal of a middle school, I decided to write to him to see if he had a job for my depressed, unemployed daughter.

ZACK. And I dropped my sandwich when I saw her name appear in my inbox.

SHERRY. And I smoothed my hair down as I typed the word:

ZACK. The subject line just read:

ZACK and SHERRY. "Hi."

## Scene 11

### Sewing

*That evening.*

*Joseph sits at the table trying to thread a needle. He is finding it nearly impossible.*

*Joseph finally threads it as Zack enters.*

JOSEPH. *(To himself, triumphant.)* YES! *(Joseph proudly holds up the threaded needle.)* Zack, look! I am sewing! *(Joseph holds up a button.)* I noticed your shirt was missing a button the other day and we can't have that, now can we? *(Zack looks for something in a draw-*

*er.)* What are you looking for?

ZACK. Nothing. *(Zack rummages around until he finds two hammers. He silently puts them down the back of his pants while Joseph concentrates on his threaded needle. He decides to back up out of the room so that Joseph won't notice the hammers.)* OK, I'll be back …

JOSEPH. *(Noticing Zack's weird walk.)* Zack?

ZACK. What?

JOSEPH. It's just. You look a little, uh, happy. Did something good happen today?

ZACK. No. *(Zack continues committing to his backwards exit smiling at Joseph who stares at him, confused. Once he is alone again, Joseph pulls the thread through the button and it comes right out of the shirt because he doesn't know to knot the thread. Joseph stares at the needle wondering what he's doing wrong.)*

## Scene 12

### The Rescue: Part 2

*A little later.*

*Sherry is asleep on the couch with Grace. It's dark. Their snoring has becoming somewhat synchronized.*

*There's a knock on the door. Sherry looks up and sees Zack as a shadowy figure in the window holding two hammers.*

SHERRY. *(Frightened.)* Gah! *(Sherry realizes it's just Zack and goes to the door, turning on the light.)* Zack? *(Zack enters.)*

ZACK. Were you sleeping? It's like seven o'clock. *(Zack holds up the hammers, excited.)* Hammers! *(Zack heads for the basement door.)*

SHERRY. Huh?

ZACK. We're gonna need to smash that lock. *(Zack goes over to the basement door. He raises the hammer to bang on the lock. Sherry is quick to stop him.)*

SHERRY. Wait! We can't! *(Gesturing to Grace.)* She'll wake up.

ZACK. I really don't care. *(Zack offers Sherry his other hammer.)* Here, take your best swing. *(Sherry takes the hammer.)*

SHERRY. OK! *(Sherry daintily taps the lock while Zack watches.)*

ZACK. So you've seen someone use a hammer before, right?

SHERRY. If I hit it much louder she'll wake up.

ZACK. Wait — I've got an idea. *(Zack goes to the television and turns on* Top Gun. *"Danger Zone" plays loudly. Grace wakes up briefly. Zack and Sherry freeze in fear of being caught. Grace just looks at the TV, registers that* Top Gun *is playing — all is well — she moves her head to the music as she falls back asleep. Zack shouts over the music.)* OK, come on, on the count of three. One! Two! *(Zack bangs on the lock with his hammer. Sherry bangs on the lock with her hammer. They continue to take turns going back and forth. The sound of barking can be heard.)*

SHERRY. AH!!!! *(Bark.)*

ZACK. Raaaaa!!! *(Bark.)*

SHERRY. AH!!!!

ZACK. RRRRAAAAAAAAA!!!!! *(Bark bark. They go on like this until the lock breaks. They rejoice.)*

| ZACK. | SHERRY. |
|---|---|
| Yeah! | Hooray! |

*(Zack continues to swing at the door with his hammer. He smashes through it and creates a large hole.)*

SHERRY. Zack! Stop! What are you doing?

ZACK. *(Panting, exhilarated.)* I don't know … I don't know …

SHERRY. *(Sherry holds up a large bag.)* We can put the dogs in here!

ZACK. *(Zack bends down into the closet and puts the dogs in the bag. Zack holds up the somewhat unwieldy bag, proudly.)* I've got them!

SHERRY. OK, let's go! *(Grace stirs.)*

GRACE. *(Groggy.)* Sherry?

SHERRY. Oh no.

GRACE. Are you having a party?

ZACK. *(To Sherry.)* You stay and distract her and I'll return the dogs, OK?

SHERRY. OK!

ZACK. *(Zack is halfway out the door when he turns back around.)* Wait, where does Troy live?

SHERRY. 112 Grove Street. Just leave the dogs in the yard.

ZACK. Got it.

SHERRY.  And call me when you're done?

ZACK.  Yeah. *(Zack goes to leave but turns back.)* Oh hey, this was fun! *(Zack exits. Sherry looks at the hole in the basement door, distressed. She looks around the room and discovers a potted plant on a stand which she moves in front of the hole — it doesn't cover it completely. Sherry stares at it for a moment and then decides that it's good enough. Sherry returns to the couch and turns off* Top Gun. *Grace wakes up, annoyed.)*

GRACE.  Hey, I was watching that. *(Grace turns an empty bottle of Jack Daniels upside down and sits under it. Sherry sits down on the couch and faces Grace.)*

SHERRY.  Grace?

GRACE.  Where'd it all go?

SHERRY.  You drank it.

GRACE.  I did?

SHERRY.  Yes. You're drunk.

GRACE.  *YOU'*re drunk.

SHERRY.  Huh?

GRACE.  Exactly!

SHERRY.  OK, we need to talk.

GRACE.  Not again. I'm fiiine, Sherry. I deleted like *two* pictures of Troy from my cellphone today.

SHERRY.  You need to return his stuff.

GRACE.  *(Grace curls up and closes her eyes.)* Keep talking, I may look like I'm asleep but I'm listening, I promise.

SHERRY.  Remember when I was sitting in bed, staring at the ceiling all day and *you* came in and put me in charge of picking out your wedding invitations?

GRACE.  I was just too lazy to do it myself.

SHERRY.  No you weren't. You put me in charge of invitations to give me something to do. I looked forward to it. You knew I needed that because you love me.

GRACE.  No, I just tricked you into doing all of the crappy work I didn't feel like doing because you're a chump.

SHERRY.  You were looking out for me. And now I'm looking out for *you*. Come on. It's been a month. He's just a man. He's just a stupid insurance salesman who cheated on you because he's an idiot and he didn't deserve you anyway. I think he actually did you a —

GRACE.  Ugh, will you just *shutthefuckupalready?!* *(Grace rolls over,*

*covering her face with pillows.)*
SHERRY. *(Sherry freezes, hurt.)* I don't even know who you are anymore. Do you know how awful that is? I want the old you back. Can you pass that message on to the old you? If she's still in there somewhere? *(Grace lets out a loud snore.)* Fine. Forget it. Have fun drooling on the couch. *(Sherry goes to leave. Grace raises her head.)*
GRACE. I slept with Mr. Cooper.
SHERRY. No. / No …
GRACE. *Yes.*
SHERRY. *Seriously?!*
GRACE. Yeah. What's the big deal?
SHERRY. I can't believe I have to — OK, so, you know that commercial you love so much? The one for adult diapers?
GRACE. With the crossing guard!
SHERRY. Mr. Cooper *is the Crossing Guard!*
GRACE. No way. The crossing guard is a woman.
SHERRY. This is a joke, right? You didn't *actually* —
GRACE. *(Drifting to sleep.)* He let me call him Troy. It was kind of nice …
SHERRY. *(A beat, then sympathetically.)* Eww … *(Sherry's cell phone rings and she picks it up.)* Hey Zack, how'd it go? What?! Oh no! Uh, alright, don't panic. I'll be right there. *(Sherry gets her coat from the closet. She grabs two flashlights. She heads for the door. The house phone rings. Sherry stares at it. She looks upstairs towards her mother's bedroom and speaks to herself.)* Sorry, Mom.

# Scene 13

## The Search

*An hour later.*

*Zack and Sherry are standing in the woods. An owl can be heard hooting. The only light is from the moon and the two flashlights Zack and Sherry carry.*

*Zack is pacing back and forth, worried.*

ZACK. If you asked me this morning: Zack, do you think you can outrun a chihuahua? My answer would have been different than it is now.

SHERRY. Come on, we'll find him. *(Calling out.)* Here dog!

ZACK. Here boy!

SHERRY. Here dog!

ZACK. Here boy! *(To Sherry.)* It just happened so fast! I got to the condo. And I thought, shit, you know, I can't just leave the dogs in the yard. So I started to open the door when a woman's voice screamed, "Who's there?" And I just panicked and dropped the bag and next thing I know, both dogs are leaping out and the bigger one is running towards the street. And I'm chasing after it. I'm chasing after this dog and I don't even know his fucking name so I can't call anything, I'm just running behind him like I'm his fucking jogging partner —

SHERRY. Did the woman in Troy's condo sound like a podiatrist?

ZACK. What?

SHERRY. Nothing.

ZACK. We *have* to find that other dog. There's a tiger roaming these streets. That little guy is in extreme danger!

SHERRY. Awww.

ZACK. What?

SHERRY. You called the chihuahua a "little guy."

ZACK. Well he is a little guy. *(Calling out.)* Here boy!

SHERRY. Don't you mean: Here, Little Guy!

ZACK. Shut up. *(A moment passes. They stand facing out, pointing their flashlights into the darkness.)*

SHERRY. *(Sigh.)* Ah … Nighttime. You know sometimes I like to go outside at night just to like, think, and stuff … *(Testing.)* Do you have any places where you like to go? To think?

ZACK. What?

SHERRY. Just like a place where you go to be alone. Like, maybe, a favorite room? In your house?

ZACK. My dad talked to you about the closet.

SHERRY. No.

ZACK. Don't lie to me. How do you expect me to trust you if you just lie to me?

SHERRY. Look, obviously I talk to your dad — he's my boss and he's concerned.

ZACK. Yeah, well he's the one who should be in therapy.

SHERRY. Yeah? Do you ever think about how he's feeling?

ZACK. Wow — there was so much judgment in that question.

SHERRY. Well, do you?

ZACK. I'm like, covered in your judgment right now.

SHERRY. Your dad is running a whole school. And he's trying to keep his family together. It's really hard trying to keep a family together, trust me. And I know you're sad about your mom, but your dad is probably just as sad and I just think that maybe the two of you could get through it together as opposed / to —

ZACK. I drove my mom into a tree. There, there you go. That's what happened. It was raining. I lost control of the car and swerved. And because of some self-preservation instinct I swerved the car, *on purpose,* to the passenger side so that she was the one whose entire body was broken. She didn't even die right away. *(Zack stares at the ground.)* I feel like I'm gonna puke.

SHERRY. It's OK to cry. If you're crying it's probably because you —

ZACK. *(Quietly.)* Please stop talking. *(They stand in silence for a moment.)* This is useless. I'm going home. *(Zack exits. Sherry watches him leave.)*

# Scene 14

## Yoga

*Later that night.*

*Joseph stands in front of the dining room table holding a copy of a yoga magazine.*

*He is on the telephone.*

JOSEPH. *(Speaking very clearly.)* Cancel My Subscription. *(After a moment he says this more clearly.)* Cancel. My. Subscription. *(After a moment he screams into the phone.)* CANCEL MY SUBSCRIPTION! *(He waits while he's connected to an operator.)* Hi. I'd like to cancel my subscription. Yeah. Uh-huh. Um, yes the subscription number is ... *(He looks at the cover.)* 354H as in hhhhamburger? — 678B as in bellicose? — 28G as in goblins! — 4. Yes, it's addressed to my wife but it's on my credit card. Yes, even if it was *free* she would still be completely uninterested in receiving it. *(Pause.)* A reason? I don't know, because she just doesn't want it. *(Zack enters the house holding his flashlight. It's still on. He stops for a moment and takes in Joseph's phone conversation.)* OK, well guess what, OK, get ready because I'm gonna tell you something: it's possible for one woman to realize that she *doesn't like yoga.* Yeah, she hates it. *(Zack exits.)* When this month's issue came she looked at it and was like "Oh. God." And then she walked over to the window, opened it up and threw the magazine out of it. *(Pause.)* Yes, I realize that, but what if it's the yoga that's making her angry in the first place?! *(Zack reenters with a box of cookies and a glass of milk. He sits down at the table to eat his cookies as he continues to watch Joseph.)* Would you ever pick up a brand new, pristine copy of the magazine, hot off the presses, and immediately throw it in the garbage!? *(Starting to crack.)* Because that's what you're doing every month by continuing to send my wife this magazine. *(Joseph takes a deep breath.)* Thank you. *(Joseph slams the phone down. He looks at Zack eating a cookie. Zack looks up and sees Joseph looking at him.)*

## Scene 15

## You Really Have a Rifle

*The following Tuesday. At the school. Sherry enters Joseph's office and sees him sitting at his desk, examining his rifle.*

SHERRY. You really have a rifle. I thought that was a joke.
JOSEPH. Nope. This is my rifle. I need it for protection. There's a tiger roaming the streets, young lady!
SHERRY. It's been weeks, don't you think the tiger has like, I don't know, moved on?
JOSEPH. Until the tiger is apprehended it could be anywhere. And we need to protect ourselves.
SHERRY. To tell you the truth, I kinda forget about it most of the time.
JOSEPH. Oh, you'll forget about it right until it jumps out right in front of you. *(Joseph suddenly jumps up and screams.)* AARGH! *(Sherry screams.)*
JOSEPH. Like that.
SHERRY. Anyway … the reason I'm here is because Zack hasn't shown up for work the last few days.
JOSEPH. Oh yes, he's sick.
SHERRY. Really?
JOSEPH. Yes. Is everything going OK in class? Is he giving you any trouble?
SHERRY. No, no, he's fine.
JOSEPH. I think he really likes this job.
SHERRY. Yeah?
JOSEPH. He's been ironing his shirts.
SHERRY. Oh.
JOSEPH. I've never seen him do that.
SHERRY. Well, you never know, maybe all these years he's been a

*closet ironer. (Awkward pause.)*
JOSEPH. You know, it really is remarkable how much you resemble your mother when she was younger.
SHERRY. Oh, I don't really.
JOSEPH. No, you look like her in a lot of ways — the way your nose tilts slightly to the left ... *(Remembering.)* Your mother was the most beautiful girl in school. *(Studying Sherry a little closer.)* Hmm ... I guess you don't look like her *that much.*
SHERRY. *(Getting up.)* Oook ... well —
JOSEPH. Everyone wanted to date Wanda. But she chose me. I remember feeling *so lucky.* I'm sure your father feels the same way.
SHERRY. I don't think he was feeling very *lucky* when he decided to just leave in the middle of the night and not come back.
JOSEPH. What?
SHERRY. About a month ago — he just left. You didn't — ?
JOSEPH. I had no idea. What happened?
SHERRY. Ah, I probably shouldn't —
JOSEPH. No, tell me. Please?
SHERRY. Well ... OK. So, my mom has this illness?
JOSEPH. Oh god. Is it serious?
SHERRY. No one really knows. But she's been taking this medicine that's made her ...
JOSEPH. What?
SHERRY. Fat?
JOSEPH. So she's ... fat?
SHERRY. Yeah. And she won't let anyone see her. *I* haven't even seen her in months. She's just been hiding in her room. But I figure *she has to come out eventually, right?*
JOSEPH. So you're not *trying* to get her out?
SHERRY. Of course I'm trying, but it has to be her decision.
JOSEPH. That's a rather passive way of looking at it, don't you think? She needs someone to go up there and rescue her from herself.
SHERRY. Do *you* want to try?
JOSEPH. Me? I can't.
SHERRY. Right. Well, tell Zack I hope he feels better. *(Turns to leave, then turns back.)* Oh, and my mother says, "Remember Harold Ashman's pants?" (Joseph laughs, softly at first, but eventually after a few moments, he is howling in a fit of uncontrollable laughter. Sherry laughs nervously.) Yeah. OK, then ... byyyye ... (Sherry leaves as Joseph continues laughing.)

# Scene 16

## Walgreens

*Later that afternoon.*

*Sherry enters Walgreens and sees Zack putting price tags on lipsticks.*

SHERRY. *(Sarcastic.)* That's a good shade for you. *(Zack looks up, surprised to see Sherry, then immediately turns away from her and focuses on the lipstick.)*

ZACK. I need to make sure they have price tags. Our scanner's broken.

SHERRY. Oh! Is scanning the most fun part of the job? I always imagined it would be either that or using the intercom.

ZACK. What do you want?

SHERRY. Well first, I want to know how you're feeling. I heard you were too sick to come to work.

ZACK. Uh-huh.

SHERRY. I haven't seen you since we returned Troy's dogs.

ZACK. Don't you mean *dog?*

SHERRY. Right. Anyway, class has been going well. No one's climbed out the window this week!

ZACK. Congratulations.

SHERRY. Can you look at me?

ZACK. I'm working. I don't come into your place of work and start disrupting things, do I?

SHERRY. Actually …

ZACK. Well, don't worry, you're not going to see me there ever again. I wouldn't set foot in there if you paid me, which by the way, my dad never did even though he told me I'd be getting a paycheck which, by the way, was the only reason I was showing up. So that was a complete fucking waste of time.

SHERRY. How can you say that? Every kid has a popsicle stick basketball hoop. Some even have *two. (Zack continues to ignore her*

45

*and focus on the lipsticks.)* Zack. The other night. What you told me? About your mother…?

ZACK. Will you please get out of my Walgreens?

SHERRY. No.

ZACK. Get out of my Walgreens!!!

SHERRY. No!

ZACK. GET OUT OF MY WALGREENS!

SHERRY. No. We need to talk.

ZACK. *(Desperate.)* If I give you some lipstick will you leave?

SHERRY. Fine, I'll agree to leave if *you* agree to complete just one of the journal assignments for our next session.

ZACK. Did you not hear me before? I quit.

SHERRY. You can't quit.

ZACK. Yes I can. I fucking quit.

SHERRY. Why?

ZACK. Why not?

SHERRY. Because. You just can't, OK? Please? You can't. This is the first job I've ever had and I can't just like completely fail at it. I won't be able to handle that. I need you to help me know if I'm a good art therapist.

ZACK. You *need* me?

SHERRY. Yes.

ZACK. Well that is massively unfair. I'm pretty sure the last thing anyone wants is a needy therapist.

SHERRY. I know. *(Sherry looks away, trying not to cry.)*

ZACK. *(Softening a little bit.)* Um, I'm gonna go back to work now. OK?

SHERRY. Yeah. OK. *(Zack exits. Sherry speaks to herself.)* I'm really sorry.

## Scene 17

### Dad

*Sherry addresses the audience.*

SHERRY. This is the story of why my dad left … *(Sherry looks at the audience for an uncomfortable moment. She doesn't know what to say. Finally she gives up.)* Yeah, I don't know.

# Scene 18

## The Tom Cruise Spot

*That evening.*

*Grace enters the living room wearing her wedding veil and holding a tin of chocolate cake.*

*She sits on the couch.*

*She begins eating the cake while simultaneously pressing play on* Top Gun. *We hear "Take My Breath Away."*

*Sherry enters and stands in front of the television.*

GRACE. Move or I will kill you.
SHERRY. I have to tell you something.
GRACE. *Sit. Down. (Sherry sits down. Grace takes the remote and attacks the volume button until we hear "Take My Breath Away" at full blast. The two women tilt their heads at the same angle. They start to sing along with the song, getting lost in the moment. Grace puts her arm around Sherry.)*
GRACE. It's good to have you back, Sherry. *(Sherry stops cold.)*
SHERRY. *(To herself.)* No! *(Sherry snaps out of it and turns the movie off. shuddering.)* Ugh. OK, that's enough. *(Sherry stands up.)* Grace, I need to show you something. *(Sherry goes over to the basement door. She moves the potted plant and opens the door, gesturing inside. Grace stares blankly, confused.)* The dogs, Grace. The DOGS.
GRACE. Oh my god! The dogs! I forgot about them!
SHERRY. I know you did!
GRACE. Oh god, I haven't fed them in days. They're gonna be dead. Shit. I killed his dogs. Aaah crap, I *really* wanted to feel

morally superior to him.

SHERRY. You didn't kill them.

GRACE. Really?

SHERRY. I returned them. Well, one of them. The other one is … at large.

GRACE. Which one?

SHERRY. The bigger one.

GRACE. *(A little sad.)* Anus.

SHERRY. That was his name?

GRACE. *(Nostalgic.)* That's what I called him. Oh god. I'm going to hell. *(Grace curls into a ball on the couch. Sherry puts her hand on Grace's back.)*

SHERRY. No you're not. You're just going through a dark time. You're not yourself.

GRACE. I don't know who I am without him.

SHERRY. Well I do. *(Exceedingly cheerfully.)* You're the *coolest big sister ever! (Grace groans into a pillow, in pain.)* Grace? *(Grace picks her head up.)*

GRACE. I'm sorry I called you a chump. I knew you'd like making the invitations.

SHERRY. I know you did.

GRACE. They were beautiful invitations.

SHERRY. *(Upbeat.)* I *really* still think we can reuse them if you marry someone whose first name starts with a T.

GRACE. I'm never going to get married. I'm never going to meet anyone. I slept with a senior citizen. *I hate myself!*

SHERRY. The whole problem here is your perception of who Troy is. You just have to change the way you think about him. Shift gears.

GRACE. How?

SHERRY. OK, well I've actually been thinking of something that might help. Close your eyes. Just do it. *(Grace closes her eyes.)* Now, picture the credits for *Top Gun* …

GRACE. That's easy.

SHERRY. I know it is. Now you need to move Troy's name out of the Tom Cruise spot. And put him in like the Val Kilmer spot. OK? He needs to go from Maverick to Ice Man. From leading man to minor supporting role. *(Pause. Grace opens her eyes wide.)*

GRACE. That. Made. *So much sense.*

SHERRY. Really?

GRACE. Yeah. It's like the first thing that's made sense in weeks! *(The doorbell rings.)*
SHERRY. OK, now hold onto that thought. Don't let it go. *(Sherry answers the door. Zack enters. He has a bloody lip and a black eye. He bounds into the room, excited.)* Oh my god. What happened?
ZACK. I can't go home because my dad will freak out if he sees me.
SHERRY. Were you mugged?
ZACK. No. But I did punch out my boss at Walgreens!
SHERRY. Why?
ZACK. I'm a little worried because I've been banned from working at CVS *and* Walgreens. I don't want to have to work in the food service industry. I really like the drugstore industry.
SHERRY.. Why did you punch him?
GRACE. Sherry, guess what?
SHERRY. What?
GRACE. It's been over a minute and he's still in the Val Kilmer spot! *(Zack heads for the couch. He points to Grace.)*
ZACK. *(Excited.)* Well, look who's vertical!
GRACE. Sack, you're really lucky to have Sherry working with you — she is an amazing and wise woman.
SHERRY. Thank you.
GRACE. It's hard to believe she's never had a boyfriend.
ZACK. *(Laughing.)* What? *(Sherry pulls Zack off the couch.)*
SHERRY. OK! Zack I'm gonna drive you home now.
ZACK. *(To Sherry.)* You've *never* had a boyfriend?
GRACE. Never.
ZACK. *(To Sherry.)* Seriously?
SHERRY. Grace, I'll be back soon!
ZACK. *(To Sherry.)* Never? (Sherry pushes Zack out the door.)
SHERRY. Come on! *(They exit. After a moment Grace picks up her phone and dials.)*
GRACE. *(Into the phone.)* Oh hey, Troy, it's Grace. I see you've decided not to pick up. Which is actually perfect because I'm just calling to say that I — *(Deep breath.)* shit — I just wish that you from 4 years ago was here, except I can't talk to that guy anymore, because in some twisted cosmic joke that guy ended up turning into you and you're like the *biggest idiot of all time!* Seriously, *what the fuck is wrong with you?* I took so *many things* from the condo! I took *the dogs!* Do you really care about not facing me more than

you care about your own dogs? What kind of person doesn't try to get his dogs back after his jilted fiancee kidnaps them? That's really sick, Troy. Anyway. *(With gravity.)* Please Continue To *Not* Contact Me. *(Grace takes a deep breath.)* Goodbye. *(Grace hangs up the phone.)*

## Scene 19

## The Shoe Closet

*Sherry and Zack sit in his mom's shoe closet.*

*Sherry puts cover up makeup on Zack's eye.*

ZACK. So have you *really never* had a boyfriend?

SHERRY. Can you please forget you heard that?

ZACK. I get it, you're just like, really selective.

SHERRY. *(Applying makeup.)* Hold still. You know, even if I do an amazing job with this, he'll still be able to see that something's wrong.

ZACK. Not if I never turn my face around.

SHERRY. You think you could spend the next week only looking at him in profile?

ZACK. Absolutely. Yes. *(A beat, then.)* I was the county hurdling champion — did you know that?

SHERRY. Um, no.

ZACK. And I had this like, yeah I guess you could call it a, *relationship*, with one of the, um, lady hurdlers. There was a lot of pressure for us to get together. Within the community. *(He remembers her.)* She could jump so high. She's the only girl I've ever dated. So you shouldn't feel bad about never dating anyone. Although you're like *a lot older than me* aren't / you?

SHERRY. OK, DONE. *(Sherry holds up a mirror.)* Tada!

ZACK. *(Looking at his reflection.)* Hey! Not bad! And to show my appreciation … *(Zack reaches into his backpack.)* Here. *(Zack hands Sherry a big plastic bag. Sherry reaches inside and pulls out a chocolate bunny.)*

SHERRY. It's a bag of chocolate bunnies.

ZACK. I mean, think about how long ago Easter was. OK? It's been *months* and these things were *still* on the shelves. Yet when I started taking them my manager was all like, "You're planning on paying for that right?" And I was like, "No way, asshole." And then he was like, "Put the chocolate bunnies back now." And I was like, "Fucking make me, you cocksucking piece of shit." And then I punched him. And then *he* punched *me,* and started like hitting me in the face with this like economy-sized bag of Skittles? But *hello,* I still walked out of there with all the bunnies. So, I think I won that fight. *(Smiling.)* See? You can do anything if you put your mind to it.

SHERRY. You have these violent episodes. If you don't work on your self-control, people are going to start thinking of you as "The guy who has those violent episodes."

ZACK. Well, that would be better than "The guy who drove his mom into a tree." *(Zack shifts nervously and looks around the closet.)* The funny thing is she had all of these shoes but she always just wore these. *(Zack holds up a pair of tennis shoes.)* She wore the same dirty sneakers every day but she was holding onto all of these beautiful, fancy shoes — the whole time they were just sitting in here, like trophies. Hey. What size are you? Do you want a pair?

SHERRY. Oh, um, wouldn't that be like, uh, weird?

ZACK. Dude. Whatever. Everything's weird. *(Zack reaches into a shoe box and pulls out a beautiful pair of silver shoes.)* I think these would look nice on you. *(Zack puts the shoes onto Sherry's feet.)* Perfect fit!

SHERRY. They *are* really pretty. *(Zack reaches into a shoebox and pulls out a bunch of photographs.)*

ZACK. These are our family pictures. I took them out of all the frames and albums and stuffed them into shoeboxes. My dad was just staring at my mom's picture all the time, he was like obsessed. Like paralyzed. So I took them. To help him — you know? And I've been drawing them. *(Zack reaches under a shoebox and pulls out his notebook.)* In my, uh, artist's journal? For my thoughts and drawings? *(Sherry stares at the notebook in amazement as Zack hands it to her.)* Here. *(Sherry flips through the pages.)*

SHERRY. You look like her!

ZACK. *(Excited.)* Yeah, see, that's what I think too.

SHERRY. These are …

ZACK. Yeah ... that's like a therapist's jackpot, right?

SHERRY. They're stunning. The way you've captured her, your whole family — with such ... care. It's just ...

ZACK. Sherry. What I'm about to say is going to sound cheesy but, OK, / I guess — you —

SHERRY. *(Muttering to herself, under Zack.)* Oh. What's happening.

ZACK. *(Nervous.)* — you, you make me want to steal candy for someone besides myself and that's never happened to me before. *(Sherry starts to cry.)* Ahhh, tears. Uh, I don't have any Kleenex but here ... *(Zack reaches into a shoebox and pulls out some tissue paper. He offers it to Sherry and she takes it.)*

SHERRY. *(Wiping her eyes.)* Just act like I'm not crying — OK? Just talk, just say something.

ZACK. Uh ...

SHERRY. TALK!

ZACK. OK. You know this closet? It's ridiculous — I used to get so mad about it because it's like almost the size of my bedroom. I complained about it forever. And my mom would just laugh it off and I'd get really angry. It didn't seem funny that her shoes were living better than I was — you know? But then, after everything — I just really like to sit in the closet with the shoes. It feels like something. You know? Everything else feels like nothing. *(He laughs nervously and keeps going.)* When the accident first happened I thought the only thing I could do was kill myself. But then, one day, it occurred to me that I had two options: kill myself or do something, something *so incredible* that my existence might not be this like terrible thing. So yeah, I feel like I need to do something incredible. But I can't figure out what that is. And I've been saving up my money so I can go away. But I don't know where to go. I could go to California and learn to surf. I could go to Colorado and learn to ski. I could go to Iowa and learn to grow corn. Could I be a farmer? That might be the right thing for me to do at this juncture. I don't know ... I just know that I have to disappear to *somewhere* for a little while.

SHERRY. I —

ZACK. Don't tell me not to!

SHERRY. That's not what I was going to say.

ZACK. Really?

SHERRY. Yeah.

ZACK. Oh. I just figured … I mean, *you* clearly believe in staying home. And seeing things through to the end. Even if it means completely giving up on having a personal life and like, not dating, and not having any friends your own age, and not having the job you actually want, / and —

SHERRY. OK, I get it.

ZACK. Which is something I *totally admire* by the way, in case I haven't told you that.

SHERRY. What I was *going* to say was: if you leave — make sure to call your dad. So he knows you're OK.

ZACK. Oh. We don't really do well with the phone.

SHERRY. Then write.

ZACK. What, like long, meaningful letters?

SHERRY. Like anything. Like a postcard with one word.

ZACK. One word?

SHERRY. Yes. One word is better than no words.

ZACK. Not necessarily. Like, what if my one word was "Help!" Without any context? That would be so scary! *(Sherry shakes her head.)* You know I'm right! *(Sherry smiles in spite of herself.)* Hey, did you know there are like ten songs with your name in it?

SHERRY. Really?

ZACK. Yeah, I googled it. I get mad bored at night. Here, this one's my favorite. *(Zack reaches in between the shoeboxes and turns on an iPod, which plays a song like Steve Perry's "Oh Sherrie."\*)*

SHERRY. Oh yeah — this one. I like this one.

ZACK. Me too. *(The music plays. They listen. Zack moves closer to Sherry.)* I think you're like the silver shoes.

SHERRY. What?

ZACK. I mean, shit, that was stupid. I mean … I think you're beautiful.

SHERRY. Please. I'm like a dull version of my mother. Like if you put a photograph of her in the sun for a year — you'd have me.

ZACK. Whatever. I think you're beautiful. *(Zack leans in to kiss Sherry. She moves away at the last moment.)*

SHERRY. Oh. Yeah. That's not gonna happen. *(Zack moves away and tries to play it off like no big deal.)*

ZACK. That's cool, that's cool. No worries … *(They both move their heads slightly to the beat of the music. Finally, Zack turns to*

---

\* See Special Note on Songs and Recordings on copyright page.

*Sherry trying to push through the awkwardness.)* Whattuuuup? *(The music swells as Sherry laughs.)*

## Scene 20

## The Return

*Later that night.*

*Grace stands in the middle of the living room, holding a clipboard. Most of Troy's things are now in shopping bags.*

*Sherry enters and cheers her on.*

SHERRY. OK! Now say each item out loud like it's a butterfly that you're releasing back into nature!
GRACE. OK! *(Grace starts to check items off of the list on her clipboard.)* His Wii. His Playstation. His Sega Genesis. His Game Cube. His Atari. All of the controllers. Most of the video games. His alarm clock. Like five electric toothbrushes. His baseball card collection. His football jersey. His socks. His pajamas. His rug. His placemats. His spice rack *and* the spices. His orthodics. His Swedish neck pillow. His George Foreman grill. His *Serpico* poster. His high school yearbook. His bathroom doorknob. His curtains. His bowls. His resume paper. His international beer bottles. His prescription goggles. His tax returns. His golf clubs. His mittens and hats. His keychain. And his key. Oh, wait! *(Grace pulls a small object out from under the couch cushion.)* And his retainer. *(Grace spits into the retainer case and puts it in a bag.)*
SHERRY. Woohoo! Now, is this everything?
GRACE. Yes! Oh. *(Grace glances sadly at the karaoke machine.)* His karaoke machine. *(Grace looks at Sherry with a pleading expression.)*
SHERRY. Wait, you can't give that back. It's too awesome!
GRACE. *(Jumping for joy and hugging Sherry.)* Thank you!!! *(Sherry helps Grace pile all of the bags on top of her shoulders and in her arms.)*

SHERRY. See? Now don't you feel better? Like a great weight has been lifted off your shoulders? *(Grace moves slowly under all of the weight.)*

GRACE. Yes…? *(Grace heads out the door.)*

SHERRY. *(Calling after her.)* Good luck!

## Scene 21

## The Escape

*Zack addresses the audience.*

ZACK. *(Excited and intense.)* This is how it happens. I wait until my dad has gone into his room for the night and then I grab the suitcase that's been sitting under my bed, packed, for months. Then I go to the kitchen to grab a box of cookies and leaning up against the leg of the table I see the rifle. And for the first time it hits me: *My dad has a rifle.* And that's not OK. He needs someone to take it away. So I do that. I walk out of the house I've lived in my whole life with a rifle, most of my belongings and a box of cookies and I have no idea if I have the courage to go any further than the town pond, which is where I'm standing, looking at the ducks when I hear it: a soft rumbling, a growling. And I turn around. And there it is. The tiger. At the town pond. And I'm, like, *armed,* you know? And I think — *I can be the guy who defended the town from the tiger!* And I'm about to pull the trigger when everything just becomes really, *really* still. I stare into the tiger's big, yellow eyes and I swear it's like he wants me to shoot him. He's tired. And alone. And lost. And I think: yeah, sure this tiger's dangerous — but like if you really think about it, who isn't? And he squints and stares at me in this sad, broken way and in that moment, for him, I choose life. I slowly lower the gun and as I do the tiger glares at me like, "Oh great. Thanks for nothing, asshole." And he just turns around and walks away. So then I'm just standing there, thinking to myself, "Now what?" When suddenly I drop the rifle and it goes off at my feet and at the sound of the gunshot I run. I run as fast I can. Suitcase and everything. I run until I'm at the bus station and then I get on a bus and then I get on another bus. *(Proud.)* And That's How I Escape.

## Scene 22

## The Rescue: Part 3

*Two weeks later.*

*Sherry is straightening up the living room when the house phone rings.*

SHERRY. *(Into the phone.)* Hi Mom. *(Pause.)* Ummm … *(Sherry goes to look out the window.)* Yes, it is. *(Pause.)* Yep, he's just sitting in there. *(Pause.)* I don't know. His appointment isn't for another minute, so I guess he wants to be exactly on time. *(Pause.)* Yeah, see? He's getting out now. *(Sherry sees something amazing.)* Oh my god. WOW! Uh, sorry Mom I gotta go, bye! *(There is a knock on the door. Sherry answers it. In the doorway, Joseph appears wearing an ill-fitting tuxedo. He is carrying flowers and a crown.)*
SHERRY. Wow!
JOSEPH. Oh. Am I early for our session?
SHERRY. No you're right on time. Come in …
JOSEPH. Alright. *(Joseph enters the house. He sits down on the couch. He takes a butterscotch out of his pocket.)* Butterscotch?
SHERRY. Sure. *(Sherry takes the candy, unwraps it and chews on it while Joseph takes a deep breath.)*
JOSEPH. So. I did the assignment. *(Joseph pulls out a notebook.)* I drew a house, like you asked.
SHERRY. Great! I can't wait to take a look! So, the first thing on today's agenda is a quick check-in. How are you doing today?
JOSEPH. Fine.
SHERRY. Nothing in particular you'd like to check in about?
JOSEPH. Not that I can think of.
SHERRY. OK.

JOSEPH. Oh! Well actually. There is one thing. I got a postcard in the mail today from Zack. But it's a little confusing. It just says — *(Joseph takes the postcard out of his jacket and shows it to Sherry.)*
SHERRY. *(Reading.)* Honeycomb.
JOSEPH. So I'm trying to figure out the message. Is he living with beekeepers? But I also know bears like honey. So maybe he's camping? Did you get a postcard?
SHERRY. No. But, the mail delivery around here these days is a little spotty. We have a complicated relationship with our mailman.
JOSEPH. Oh.
SHERRY. OK, well, I guess next we should dive / right into the —
JOSEPH. You're probably wondering about —
SHERRY. Yes.
JOSEPH. Right, well, I ... *(Joseph starts to cough.)*
SHERRY. Are you OK?
JOSEPH. Yes, yes ... I'm just ... *(More coughing.)*
SHERRY. Nervous?
JOSEPH. Well ...
SHERRY. You're a little nervous.
JOSEPH. I knew we should have met at *my* office.
SHERRY. You know, she's right up those stairs.
JOSEPH. Yes. I know.
SHERRY. First door on the left.
JOSEPH. Right ... OK ... here goes nothing. *(Joseph looks towards the stairs. After a moment he puts on his crown and begins to climb. "Norwegian Wood" plays. As Joseph walks up the staircase, Sherry watches and then turns to the audience.)*
SHERRY. This is The Story of How My Mother Got Out of Bed.

**End of Play**

# APPENDIX

1. The following is the script for Wanda's side of the phone conversations with Sherry and Grace.

## Scene 1

SHERRY. *(Into the phone.)* Hi Mom. *[How'd your first day go?]* It went OK, I guess. *[Did you see Joseph?]* Yeah. I saw him at this assembly about the tiger that escaped from the local zoo. *[Was his hair blonde and wavy?]* Blonde and wavy? Not exactly, kind of thin and grayish? *[Oh.]* I'm actually supposed to meet with him tomorrow. *[Tell him I said, hi.]* OK, I'll tell him. Hey, so *Jeopardy's* on — you want to challenge me? I'll go easy on you this time. *[Not tonight.]* OK, alright ... sure you don't need anything? I can come upstairs and — *[I'm fine.]* OK, no, I know, I just thought, you know, in honor of my first day of work but — [I'm tired.] I know, it's OK. *[You'll tell Joseph I said hi?]* Yeah, I'll tell him. *[You'll remember?]* I'll remember. *[OK, bye.]* Bye.

## Scene 6

GRACE. *(Into the phone.)* Hi Mom. *[What is that noise?]* Oh, I was singing. *[Oh.]* Mom, can I come to your room? *[No.]* I won't look at you. I'll just lie down on the carpet. You won't even know I'm there. Please? *[Can you keep it down? I'm trying to sleep.]* OK ... I'll keep it down. *[Thank you.]*

# Scene 7

SHERRY. *(Hesitating.)* Umm ... *(Brightly.)* Yeah OK! Just gimme a second. *(Into the phone.)* Hi Mom! Is everything OK? *[Are you going to the store anytime soon?]* *(Zack looks at his watch.)*

ZACK. Shit, I gotta get to work. *(Zack begins to gather his stuff. Sherry motions for him to wait a moment. Zack lingers and listens to Sherry's conversation.)*

SHERRY. *(Into the phone.)* Oh. Um, yeah, I'm going tonight actually. Do you want the usual stuff or something different? *[Bananas.]* Bananas. *[English muffins.]* And English muffins. Got it. *[Cinammon raisin.]* Cinammon raisin. Got it. *[Whole wheat.]* Whole wheat. OK ... Um, Mom, I'm kind of working right now. But can I call you back in a little bit? *[Sure.]* OK.

# Scene 9

SHERRY. *(Into the phone.)* Hi, Mom. How are you? *[A little gassy.]* Oh, really? Well we've got some antacid down here — do you want me to bring it in to you? *[Put it by the door.]* OK, I'll slide it under. Hey, I've officially been employed for two weeks. Pretty great, huh? *[Yes. Where's your sister?]* She's here with me. *(Looking down.)* *[What's she doing?]* She's sleeping. *[How does she look?]* Uh, she's looked better. But I think she could kill a lot of birds with one shower. *(Pause.)* Um, so look ... we really miss you, Mom. We don't care what you look like. You know that. We just want you to come downstairs. *(Pause.)* *[Did you ever tell Joseph I said hi?]* Oh, yeah, I told him. He says, "Hello." *[That's it?]* Yeah, that's it. *(Pause.)* *[Ask him if he remembers Harold Ashman's pants.]* "Harold Ashman's pants?" — What does that mean? *[(Laughing.) He'll know, just tell him.]* *(Laughing.)* OK, I'll just tell him. *[(Still laughing.) OK. Bye.]* OK. Bye.

# Scene 22

SHERRY. *(Into phone.)* Hi Mom. [Is that Joseph's car in our driveway?] Ummm ... *(Sherry goes to look out the window.)* Yes, it is. *[Is he just sitting in his car?]* Yep, he's just sitting in there. *[Why's he doing that?]* I don't know. His appointment isn't for another minute, so I guess he wants to be exactly on time. *[Oh.]* Yeah, see? He's getting out now. *(Seeing something amazing.)* Oh my god. WOW! Uh, sorry Mom I gotta go bye!

2. The following is the text for Joseph's optional PA announcements.

## Transition Announcement into Scene 8:

JOSEPH'S VOICE. Attention. This is Principal Moore. Will all lunch monitors please report to my office. Immediately.

## Transition Announcement into Scene 15:

JOSPEH'S VOICE. Attention. This is Principal Moore. There will be an eighth period buddy drill. Attendance is mandatory. For those of you not sure what mandatory means, it means it is *required* and you need to take it *seriously* and not just *miss it like yesterday.* OK?

# PROPERTY LIST

Microphone
Box of (extra large, odor-protectant) tampons
Bottle of Jack Daniels
Spice rack
Tissues
Candy wrappers
Backpack
Notebook
Agenda
Popsicle sticks
Papers including ink blots
*Everyone Poops* (book)
Picture of Troy
TV remote
Paper basket
Orange tissue paper
Sandwich
Butterscotch
Dinner dish, with spinach
Dog food
Kleenex
Hairpin
Blanket
Two crowns
Needle and thread
Button
2 hammers
2 chihuahuas
Large bag
Potted plant on a stand
Coat
2 flashlights
Yoga magazine
Box of cookies
Glass of milk
Rifle
Lipstick
Price labeller

Makeup
Wedding veil
Tin of chocolate cake
Pillow
Big plastic bag
Chocolate bunny
Tennis shoes
Silver shoes
Shoebox
Photographs
Tissue paper
iPod
Clipboard
Pen
Retainer in case
Many grocery shopping bags
Flowers
Notebook
Postcard

# SOUND EFFECTS

Error beep from a cash register scanner
Crowd of kids cheering (from Depends commercial/television)
Dogs barking
Dog claws on the door
Recorded voicemail message for Troy
House phone ring
Door knock
Cell phone ring
Owl hooting

# NEW PLAYS

★ **CLYBOURNE PARK by Bruce Norris.** WINNER OF THE 2011 PULITZER PRIZE AND 2012 TONY AWARD. Act One takes place in 1959 as community leaders try to stop the sale of a home to a black family. Act Two is set in the same house in the present day as the now predominantly African-American neighborhood battles to hold its ground. "Vital, sharp-witted and ferociously smart." –*NY Times.* "A theatrical treasure…Indisputably, uproariously funny." –*Entertainment Weekly.* [4M, 3W] ISBN: 978-0-8222-2697-0

★ **WATER BY THE SPOONFUL by Quiara Alegría Hudes.** WINNER OF THE 2012 PULITZER PRIZE. A Puerto Rican veteran is surrounded by the North Philadelphia demons he tried to escape in the service. "This is a very funny, warm, and yes uplifting play." –*Hartford Courant.* "The play is a combination poem, prayer and app on how to cope in an age of uncertainty, speed and chaos." –*Variety.* [4M, 3W] ISBN: 978-0-8222-2716-8

★ **RED by John Logan.** WINNER OF THE 2010 TONY AWARD. Mark Rothko has just landed the biggest commission in the history of modern art. But when his young assistant, Ken, gains the confidence to challenge him, Rothko faces the agonizing possibility that his crowning achievement could also become his undoing. "Intense and exciting." –*NY Times.* "Smart, eloquent entertainment." –*New Yorker.* [2M] ISBN: 978-0-8222-2483-9

★ **VENUS IN FUR by David Ives.** Thomas, a beleaguered playwright/director, is desperate to find an actress to play Vanda, the female lead in his adaptation of the classic sadomasochistic tale *Venus in Fur.* "Ninety minutes of good, kinky fun." –*NY Times.* "A fast-paced journey into one man's entrapment by a clever, vengeful female." –*Associated Press.* [1M, 1W] ISBN: 978-0-8222-2603-1

★ **OTHER DESERT CITIES by Jon Robin Baitz.** Brooke returns home to Palm Springs after a six-year absence and announces that she is about to publish a memoir dredging up a pivotal and tragic event in the family's history—a wound they don't want reopened. "Leaves you feeling both moved and gratifyingly sated." –*NY Times.* "A genuine pleasure." –*NY Post.* [2M, 3W] ISBN: 978-0-8222-2605-5

★ **TRIBES by Nina Raine.** Billy was born deaf into a hearing family and adapts brilliantly to his family's unconventional ways, but it's not until he meets Sylvia, a young woman on the brink of deafness, that he finally understands what it means to be understood. "A smart, lively play." –*NY Times.* "[A] bright and boldly provocative drama." –*Associated Press.* [3M, 2W] ISBN: 978-0-8222-2751-9

**DRAMATISTS PLAY SERVICE, INC.**
440 Park Avenue South, New York, NY 10016  212-683-8960  Fax 212-213-1539
postmaster@dramatists.com  www.dramatists.com